WITH UNCOMMON GRIEF

A Life Long Journey With Mental Illness

Shawn Gregory

authorHOUSE

AuthorHouse™
1663 Liberty Drive
Bloomington, IN 47403
www.authorhouse.com
Phone: 1-800-839-8640

© 2010 Shawn Gregory. All rights reserved.

No part of this book may be reproduced, stored in a retrieval system, or transmitted by any means without the written permission of the author.

First published by AuthorHouse 4/16/2010

ISBN: 978-1-4490-1025-6 (e)
ISBN: 978-1-4490-1023-2 (sc)
ISBN: 978-1-4490-1024-9 (hc)

Library of Congress Control Number: 2010901118

Printed in the United States of America
Bloomington, Indiana

This book is printed on acid-free paper.

"Scripture taken from the NEW AMERICAN STANDARD BIBLE R, Copyright C 1960, 1962, 1963, 1971, 1972, 1973, 1975, 1977, 1995 By The Lockman Foundation. Used by permission."

DEDICATION

I would like to honor my brother, who at the age of nine lost his life in a tragic accident. His life and death will always be a part of me in this world and the world to come. This book is also dedicated to my sister Eudora and my wife Reba for their constant support in helping me edit a manuscript that made dealing with uncommon grief more coherent. I would also like to thank my sister Penny, my daughter Elise, and my cousin Denny, who supported my endeavor. I have also learned to appreciate all my acquaintances in life while dealing "with uncommon grief."

CONTENTS

FOREWORD — xi

INTRODUCTION — xiii

2009 — 1
Reflections of a Recovery — 3

1952–1963 — 7
Becoming Emotionally Conscious — 9
Jeff's and My Bedroom — 14
Jeff's Accidents — 17
John Fitzgerald Kennedy — 20

1963–1970 — 23
The Accident — 25
Closer to God Than Me — 30
My Mother and the Bible — 36
Recovering the Best I Could — 39
Victories and Defeats — 42

1970–1977 — 45
Dating — 47
Wrestling with God — 51
Our Marriage — 54
My First Divorce — 57
The First Year Alone — 59

1977–1984 — 63
Fully Ashamed — 65
Mental Asylum Admission — 68

First Series of Shock Treatments	72
Second Series of Shock Treatments	77
Jean and College	80
My Second Therapist	82
Breaking Up and PSU Hospital	84
First Out-of-Body Experience	89
Suicide	91
Two Christian Girls	97
Sharon and Elizabeth	100
Sharon's Family	103
1984–1991	**105**
My Daughter Elise	107
My Fourth Therapist	109
1991–1998	**113**
My Father's Death	115
The Road to Sardis (Damascus)	118
Graduating from College	121
Heart Surgery	123
1998–Present	**127**
My Second Divorce	129
Reba	132
Reflections and Hope	135
A Validation	137
Epilogue	141
About the Author	143

FOREWORD

This book will take you on my life's journey, which has shaped my present being. It is meant to offer hints for survival techniques when dealing "with uncommon grief."

I have found that writing down these accounts became very therapeutic and healing for me. The final dreams, logged in the last chapter, happened after I finished the book. I thought this dream would have concluded my illness, but I later found out differently. My journey with my illness continues on. My most recent diagnosis was PTSD (posttraumatic stress disorder) in 1999. The event causing my disorder happened the day of John Fitzgerald Kennedy's funeral in 1963. I have suffered through many years carrying the baggage of grief. It was not till the late seventies that I began a journey of dealing with it through professional counseling. The journey is and was long but continues to be a bittersweet experience.

INTRODUCTION

The most important part of my healing process with mental illness is taking responsibility for my actions and feelings. At the beginning of my journey, after my brother died, I found many excuses to be who I was and what I was becoming. After many years of therapy, both verbal and biochemical, it made no difference how I got to being mentally ill. It became very clear once my emotions were communicated in therapy that the goal was getting out of the hole of depression. How I got there made no difference. No blame was necessary anymore; just forgiveness for myself and others. With an attitude of long-suffering and perseverance, a ladder of recovery was made available by my Lord above.

CHAPTER 1
2009

'For I came to Set A Man Against His Father, And A Daughter Against Her Mother, And A Daughter-In-Law Against Her Mother-In-Law; and A Man's Enemies Will Be The Members Of His Household.'

MATTHEW 10:35

Reflections of a Recovery

Many of my emotional wounds have healed, but scars remain that are sensitive to the continual stresses of life. Just as most physical scars are permanent, I have accepted that some of my emotional scars are permanent. Some fade with time and some don't. Not all are negative. Be they physical or emotional, not all are apparent. Even my physical body has scars and breaks from the trauma that I have encountered dealing with mental illness. My most recent diagnosis relative to modern psychology is posttraumatic stress disorder (PTSD) as a result of the earlier crises in my life. I have also been diagnosed and was treated in my early years for manic depression and reactive schizophrenia. I've come to believe that I was misdiagnosed several times in my early psychiatric evaluations. Maybe psychologists just had to define or create a new name for an old illness; I don't know. I don't believe that in the early eighties PTSD was identified or even established as a condition.

While trying to survive mental illness, the most significant trait that I developed through the years has been the ability to persevere. I had one dream in which I was carrying a tetrahedral trophy inscribed with the words "Acquainted with Grief" down my hometown street. The trials that have taken me from the sunny, carefree days of a nearly perfect early childhood to the hallways of a mental hospital have been long, lonely, and filled with despair. One moment in time changed my life forever.

I was eleven. It literally happened with a flash, and in a flash. Forever gone were my childhood days of being happy and carefree. Prior to that moment in time, my life was very peaceful. The death of my brother in an accident, tied to the observance of a president's funeral in the year 1963, changed my delicate life for a long time to come. If my life had not been so nearly perfect up until that day, would the devastation have been less? Was it the tragedy that threw me into an emotional tailspin, or was it the events after the tragedy that nearly destroyed me? I believe the latter to be true.

To this day, my family continues to mask the dysfunctional household that we became because of that day. Oh yes, we have moved on. However, we have also covered pain and truths with religious beliefs, rituals, and preoccupations because of the lump in our throats when or if the topic ever arises.

My survival instincts led me to a psychiatrist at the age of twenty-five. Before that, I had never discussed my brother's accident with anyone. I tried to save him, but I failed. I tried to cope, but I was blamed. I buried the pain and became silent. For the next sixteen years, I never spoke of the events of that day except for one time while I was dating Samantha. I cried when discussing it with her, only mentioning that I had a brother who had died. I still could not talk about the details. I did not know how to deal with all the emotions the memory brought up in me.

On that fateful day in November of 1963, the same day as JFK's funeral, no one asked me what had happened. Getting out of school in observance of JFK's funeral would haunt me for the rest of my life. I was accused by my father of playing with fire. Later, the issue about what had happened the day of the accident was taboo. No one mentioned it or asked what had happened. I was never brave enough as a child to be able to bring up the issue and defend myself after being falsely blamed for helping cause the accident.

I spent the next forty-three years not knowing what my family thought of the circumstances of the accident. Jeff was my brother, my partner. We were cowboys and Indians, pirates and captains, best friends. He was an extension of me, almost like a twin. I felt responsible for him. Was this assumed responsibility an instinct built within my nature, or were there subtle implications from my family that caused me to carry this role? Again, I do not know. I do know this. As a cloud hung over a nation that November day in 1963, a cloud descended over my family and me; the same type of cloud—large, dark, consuming, and threatening.

In humility with and before God, I write these reflections of my life in an attempt to offer hope and encouragement to those who have suffered similar trauma and tragedies. I have gained a lot of emotional wisdom, but recovery is still an ongoing effort. My own perception in this world leads me to believe that the process of recovery may not be complete until I meet my Lord, Jesus Christ, in person.

CHAPTER 2
1952–1963

The Lord God planted a garden toward the east, in Eden; and there He placed the man whom He had formed.

GENESIS 2:8

My first approach to God was in a vegetable garden. I wondered at the age of five who He was and why He put me here. Could it be to write these chronicles of my life?

Becoming Emotionally Conscious

I was born June 10, 1952. I was my parents' first male child, with four older sisters. My earliest memories are amazing to me, not only because they summon up an extremely early period in my life, but also because they are so vivid.

I remember lying in the crib, wanting a bottle. I recall crying, wanting my hunger pangs to go away or needs met, wanting attention. I also remember having my diaper changed on Mom and Dad's bed. I remember peeing one day while I lay naked on their bed before Mom could get the diaper on me. I believe that I remember these things because it was my first emotional awareness that I had some control over my surroundings and what was happening around me. This awareness never lessened, never decreased at all. I've always had a high conscience level in life, a very sensitive nature.

When I was a toddler I was walking in the vegetable garden one day and looked up to the sky and wondered why God had put me here and also wondered about Him. Later I would sing "O My Papa" on my father's lap. I was blessed with having a good family.

It was not uncommon through the years for topics of conversations to turn to God and/or religion. Much later in my life when my daughter Elise observed them, she labeled these conversations as "God-ding." These conversations were sometimes discussions and sometimes questions of or about God. These were not questions in a way to doubt His authority but an attempt to understand His ways. I believe my questioning or "God-ding" was initiated before my classes in Catholicism began in the first grade.

I started a love/hate relationship with the church at an early age. Naturally, I can recall my first Catholic catechism class. It was to be immediately after church services. After the mass I went to the car and locked myself in to try to keep my parents from making me go to class. They gave me an ultimatum: open the door or have a whipping. Refusing to attend class was not an option. After some deliberation I opened the door and got out. Finally, in fear, I walked into church by myself and sat in the class. I felt very afraid and ashamed. I was only six years old when I walked by myself to the front of the church where the class was meeting. It was a lonely and humiliating experience as the class stared at me walking to the altar.

My first experiences with the Catholic Church were harsh. Later in life it would become even harsher. I believe I was no closer to God in the Catholic Church than I was in the vegetable garden.

My early childhood was filled with playing with my brother Jeff, my older sisters, and the Arnolds, who lived next door. There were normal childhood issues. Around the age of six I had an intestinal blockage, and I had diarrhea for a long period of time. I recall going to the hospital and being given enemas several times a day. I was very lonely there and don't recall my family visiting me. I remember looking out into the hallway and feeling all alone while I was in the hospital with the stomach problems. I felt abandoned by my family. I also experienced this in my young adult years. The stomach cramps were horrible then and throughout my childhood years. As an adult, I figured out that I was allergic to milk and dairy products. The doctors in my childhood and adolescent years kept putting me on milk and bland diets. This is yet one more example of the failure of those whom I was trusting to help me. Not only did they fail to provide relief, but they added to my suffering. Except for short episodes of this nature, I was in a world of bliss and happiness in those bittersweet early years.

> *It is by his deeds that a lad distinguishes himself*
> *If his conduct is pure and right.*
> *The hearing ear and the seeing eye,*
> *The Lord has made both of them.*

PROVERBS 20:11–12

As children we are reprimanded by our parents when we do wrong in their eyes. I was reprimanded the day of my brother's accident for a deed I didn't commit. I found it very difficult to forgive my father for this. I hid this in my mind, after Jeff's death, planning on getting even in heaven. How, I don't know. I eventually have come to let revenge go and now just deal with forgiveness and surviving.

Shawn and Jeff

Jeff's and My Bedroom

Our bedroom was located upstairs directly above Mom and Dad's bedroom. With six children in a small house, Jeff and I had to share a double bed. The four girls, Eudora, Penny, Jane, and June, shared one room with two double beds. Jeff and I had another room. There was an external closet for Jeff and me to hang up clothes in. We also had a small chest of drawers in the room for our undergarments. There was an old book lying high on the dresser like it was supposed to be out of reach. Normal childhood curiosity led me to get the book down from the top of the dresser. There were drawings of naked men and women in it.

This was obviously a way for us to learn about sex in a strict Catholic family. I became ashamed and felt like I was doing wrong when I would read the sex manual. The feelings, though, did not stop my curiosity. I continued to learn more about what the sex act was and where babies came from. It was fascinating.

Jeff and I played hard most days. We played together, got dirty together, and bathed together. Before tiredness and family rules would send us to bed, we would gather as a family around Mom and Dad's bed and say the rosary.

Some of the Catholic rituals seemed to impose the fear of God in me. Rituals like lighting candles when there was a storm outside became a scary event. Others, such as following the "stations of the cross," were also embedded in my thinking.

How gruesome a death Christ had, I thought. It was a religious horror story. The fear of death became an emotional nightmare in my family. Later it was one of the main constituents of the dark cloud that lingered overhead.

Finally Jeff and I would go to bed. At times we held each other while we lay waiting for sleep. This was one of the best parts of the day for Jeff and me. We enjoyed napping and sleeping. I consider this to be a natural part of growing up; we were totally innocent children.

'And not only this, but we also exult in our tribulations, knowing that tribulations brings about perseverance; and perseverance, proven character; and proven character, hope.'

Romans 5:3-4

I believe that my ability to persevere was from God. He favored me in my youth and later years. He gave me strength in dealing with grief. I believe he was planning to build my character with uncommon grief. He may have taken a liking to me in the vegetable garden.

Jeff's Accidents

By the time Jeff was nine he was very outgoing. He would visit the Arnold girls and play with them in the woods and playhouses. I was more cautious and always stayed a step behind. Jeff did have a problem with accidents, though. He broke his ankle once when he jumped off my dad's dump truck. Another time he fell off the swinging gate and fractured his skull. One time we were fishing in the creek, and he cut his hand on a sharp coffee can. I sent him home. My mother scolded me when I got home, telling me he could have bled to death. I felt bad and went out in the yard by myself. Incidents like this probably contributed to my role as "the protector."

Although Jeff was accident-prone we also had some great times. We would play in the gravel pit, which was on Dad's property. We would run and slide down the gravel piles. At night we would lie on the gravel piles and watch the stars. It was overwhelming and beautiful.

There was one time when we tried to make a go-cart. It was very crude compared to today's standards, but it worked occasionally. We actually pushed it more to make it run than actually riding it. Other times we would lie on blankets under the large maple trees in our yard and take naps and daydream. Other than Jeff's tendency to have accidents, we lived in a Garden of Eden.

Jeff and Daisy

> *"The Lord your God will raise up for you a Prophet like me from among you, from your countrymen, you shall listen to him.*

Deuteronomy 18:15

From my early childhood I came to believe that John Fitzgerald Kennedy was a man sent from God.

John Fitzgerald Kennedy

While in grade school I became a gang leader to the extent of two teams fighting each other on the playground over the 1960 presidential election. I, being from a staunch Catholic family, had a strong preference for John Kennedy. I am sure the devotion to Kennedy came from the casual table talk with my family.

At school a gang was for Nixon; another gang was for Kennedy. The teams were very lopsided in numbers but more even in fighting skills. There were two boys, the Park brothers, who were for Nixon. The rest of the boys, possibly ten in number, were for Kennedy. We would go out on the playground at recess and run into each other and tackle one another. The two Nixon boys were very large and strong. They would throw the ten Kennedy boys around easily. I would stand back at times and cheer us on. Little did I know how the fate of John Kennedy would play into my brother's death.

We were let out of school early one Friday in November of 1963. Kennedy had been shot and killed in Dallas, Texas. I was stunned and very saddened by his death and also frightened. The following Monday we were also let out of school for his funeral. I thought that would be a good day.

CHAPTER 3
1963–1970

Death and life are in the power of the tongue.

Proverbs 18:21

I have become very sensitive to this verse. What people say to you can greatly affect your emotional well-being. It can also do great harm or bring great health to your psyche as you grow up. I was subject to a cloud of depression because of the power of the tongue from those most near me.

The Accident

On Monday, November 25, 1963, JFK's funeral was on TV. My whole family was watching except Jeff and me. I was playing my favorite sport behind the shed; I had a passion for basketball. All of a sudden I heard a chilling scream. It came from the barn about thirty yards away. The scream and sight were horrifying ... Jeff was running up the sidewalk ... A five-foot flame was trailing behind him ... He was on fire ... His winter coat was totally engulfed in flames ... He was screaming and running ... I dropped the ball and became numb ... I immediately tried to run to him but was scared ... It seemed like forever getting to him ... Time was in slow motion ... I finally reached him at the end of the walkway ... I tackled him and threw him to the ground ... He was face down ... I started beating the flames out on his back with my bare hands ... Simultaneously I tried to yell for help. I couldn't speak ...

This was the most psychological trauma that I could have experienced as an eleven-year-old. I believe it caused me to split psychologically from right brain to left in my adult years. The results of this would be labeled by the PSU doctors as reactive schizophrenia under stress and later PTSD.

My sister Penny came out of the house about seventy yards away. I finally was able to scream, "Help me!"

Mother came running out of the house, followed by the rest of those who were at home at the time. Mother grabbed

Jeff from me and held him close. When she grabbed him from me, she gave me the impression that I had done something wrong. She looked at me with anger.

Mother started crying heavily. She had gotten burned from clutching him so close. Someone in the family ran and got a blanket from the house. They took him to the car. Someone else called for an ambulance. Forty years afterward I learned which sister called the ambulance: Penny.

I went and sat on the porch at the house … I was still in shock … Dad came up on the porch after me. He yelled at me … "This is what you get for playing in fire!" he said angrily.

Then they took Jeff away. I felt very bad and became speechless. I feared my father before and after this. I went from being a hero to a devil in a few minutes in my mind. I felt bad for Jeff and me. I felt, if not consciously then maybe subconsciously, throughout my following childhood years that my mother and father blamed me for the accident. They would never say that, though. I was always trying to read their minds and emotions. I didn't know how they felt about me … Because of the lack of communication, my assumptions became my reality. In my madness I never spoke of the accident out loud. I always consoled myself that God knew what had happened. When my relatives died they would then know what happened too. This left a deep-rooted vengeance in me. My parents clothed me and cared for me and loved me. They gave me very little emotional support in social areas in the years after Jeff's death. They actually withdrew socially too.

The attention and support that I longed for came from my sisters. They did their best. Mostly they just pampered me. They did not know how or possess the skills to help me get the anger for the loss and blame out in the open. In my youth the only social functions in our family became the Catholic Church. Being blamed for the accident and never having it resolved with my family caused me unnecessary depression with super-low self-esteem. I was always looking for approval from my peers. I became stuck in adolescence. I did not know how to deal with my situation.

Time seemed to stop that day in November of '63 … One of my twin sisters, June, came down home from town. I complained of my hands burning. She decided to take me to the hospital in her Volkswagen. I vaguely remember the trip but do remember her driving at a very high speed.

We arrived at the hospital and immediately went to the emergency room. Lying on the table was Jeff, stark naked. I felt for him as if he were being violated. This was my brother. They were administering to his burns. They directed me to a sink behind his head, and I washed my hands, which were burning.

I think subconsciously I was washing my false guilt away in tears. What guilt? I was an unspoken hero in my own eyes. This whole ordeal was very symbolic in my present thinking.

To this day I think God holds a special place for me in his eyes with Jeff. I think Jeff does too.

The medical staff applied some lotion and bandages to both of my hands. They sent me away, and I left the room. That was the last time I saw Jeff alive. June, Penny, and I left the hospital and went to June's home. I was numb and in shock the rest of the day.

That night I went to bed knowing that they were taking Jeff to PSU Hospital. I was sleeping on the couch at June's house next to the front door when Mom and Dad came in at about 2:00 AM the following morning. Mom said Jeff had gone to heaven … I started crying and cried the rest of the night in my sister's bed …

To this day, some nights I wake up with a dreaded feeling of paranoia. I feel as if someone is trying to get me. It's an unnatural fear of death. I did not talk in detail of the accident until the year 1979, sixteen years after it happened.

Now the passage of Scripture he was reading was this:

"He Was Led As A Sheep To Slaughter;
And As A Lamb Before Its Shearer Silent,
So He Does Not Open His Mouth.
"In Humiliation His Judgement Was Taken Away;
Who will Relate His Generation?
For His life Is Removed From The Earth."

Acts 8:32–33

This verse has actually comforted me at times. In a sense I felt close to Christ; even like Him. I spoke not of the accident and held it all in. I took my father's verbal punishment for Jeff's death at the age of eleven and endured the grief alone in silence.

Closer to God Than Me

The days following Jeff's death were numb and expressionless. I do remember the visits to the funeral home in the evenings. I cried a lot there. I cried with my uncle Sam. He was the only one who tried to comfort me at the funeral home. He seemed to care for me then. There were not a lot of words, just crying and listening. I remember going to church Wednesday evening at the Catholic Novena. The whole family prayed the "stations of the cross." It was very haunting, with clouds of death everywhere along with mountains of grief.

Religion became a forced passion of mine because of its association with grief. Mother insisted that I go to church every day and serve mass as an altar boy. She told me that God would reward me someday for this obedience.

Where is the good news in the church? I wondered. *I see none.* Even when you die you have to be prayed for in order to go to heaven. I truly believe that modern-day Sadducees and Pharisees like the ones who persecuted Christ still live in some churches. Some, I believe, have persecuted my soul. I continually still have trouble with churches today. My relationship with religion and churches has become a love/hate one.

After the death of my brother a great cloud of depression came over my family and me. Jeff was buried the Friday after

JFK's funeral. I may have been the altar boy for the funeral; I can't remember.

After the funeral I went home. My hands were still burning from the accident, and I was told I had to visit the doctor, the same one Jeff was with when he died going to PSU in an ambulance. He evidently inhaled flames at the accident site, and because of the burning of his lungs, he suffocated to death. No one talked of the details of this. To this day, this is all I know of why he died.

One of my sisters took me in to see the doctor. I was called into an examination room with my sister. The doctor then sent my sister out of the examination room and asked if I needed to say something. I said nothing and was still overwhelmed with shock. I returned home to the darkness. I think the doctor really cared for me, but I did not know what to say. I was still in shock.

I went back to school the following Monday and just stood in the open back closets. I was afraid to come out and face people. One schoolmate gave me some words of condolence. "I'm sorry about your brother," he said.

I said nothing but looked down and then reluctantly moved into the classroom. My social skills and self-esteem were shattered. I was suffering from an emotional breakdown at the age of eleven. Later in my school evaluations I had trouble with English and explaining myself. This has lasted a lifetime. I still deal with deciding which things I should or should not say.

Mother was hit worse by Jeff's death than I was at the time. She cried in bed a lot. Father was able to hide his grief and darkness in his work and remained active. My two oldest sisters, who were twins, Jane and June, were married and were at a distance to the grief. Jane had a son who had died at birth just a few months earlier. My middle two sisters, Eudora and Penny, were in high school and had boyfriends and school activities but were also somewhat subject to Mom's depression. Later that spring grandpa died. Three deaths in a year; mother was devastated.

Jeff's death happened over the holidays in '63, which made the grief even worse. I remember coming down to the Christmas tree that same year on Christmas morning to open the gifts. I had done this with Jeff all of our young lives. Mother was in bed crying. She said she wanted to die. Mom and Dad's bedroom was next to the living room where the Christmas tree was. I felt bad and sad. I didn't even play with the gifts that morning. To this day, mother talks very little of those memories and has filled most discussions with scripture from the Bible. She rationalizes that Jeff is the reason she is closer to God. No doubt this is true for her. However, I believe that I was much closer to God during my experience in the vegetable garden than I was performing any denominational church custom. I am not sure about me being closer to God because of Jeff's death. In reality I believe God had to become closer to me to pull me through the trials with miracles and revelations. Am I better than anyone else? No …

I recall Eudora coming to me in those days and asking how I was. I seldom responded with anything other than, "Okay."

One of my cousins said, "There is more food on the table now."

I wondered who would get Jeff's toys. I quit playing with toys and found solace in being quiet and sleeping and closing my eyes in thought and in darkness.

When I was a child I sometimes liked to just sit around and think. When the grief and darkness invaded, though, my thoughts turned against me for many years. A psychiatrist told me once that I liked being knocked out. In more recent years, though, I have begun to enjoy sitting and thinking more, so I am now able to write about these events. There were times when I could not read a paragraph in a book or comprehend what I read because of my wandering and racing thoughts.

In the months following the accident, I was extremely nervous and felt very afraid. I remember not being allowed to sleep in the bedroom upstairs that Jeff and I slept in. I no longer had the safe secure haven that I used to. It was very haunting, lonely with death. Mother hung Jeff's casket crucifix on a wall downstairs. She put his burned clothes in a drawer in her bedroom. We started to attend the Catholic mass every day. Mom and Dad gave money to the Catholic Church for a high mass for Jeff's soul salvation. Mother sang and became the church's solo organist. I was the altar boy and knelt down at the altar and responded in Latin to the priest. I never knew totally what I was saying. My knees became sore because of their sensitivity to the kneeler. I believe that this Latin language may have been the language I spoke later on the road to Sardis (Damascus) when I split mentally.

After Jeff died I initially slept downstairs in the TV room on a single bed. Dad had our property leased and mined to a local gravel company. At night when the gravel pit lights from the night shift were shining across the house I became scared that someone was going to get me. I remember sweating and being awake on these nights.

Eventually I was allowed to sleep with my sisters Eudora and Penny. The bedroom that Jeff and I slept in was now a "shadow of death." I would try and sleep with one eye on the bedroom door as I lay in bed. I felt that God and my family had abandoned me. Dark clouds were everywhere even at midday.

Children, obey your parents in the Lord, for this is right.
HONOR YOUR FATHER AND MOTHER [which is the
first commandment with a promise],
So THAT IT WILL BE WELL WITH YOU, AND THAT
YOU MAY LIVE LONG ON THE EARTH.
Fathers, do not provoke your children to anger, but
bring them up in disciple and instruction of the Lord.

EPHESIANS 6:1–4

I have always tried to honor my father and mother. Sometimes I did argue with them, usually about their beliefs or what they thought about someone. I am not sure I am honoring them with this book, though. I do honor them by being truthful with how I perceive my childhood after Jeff's death. I believe a lot of their responses to me caused my illness as a youth, which then developed into a full-blown disorder after my first divorce. My relationship with my parents developed into a love/hate relationship, as with God and religion.

My Mother and the Bible

I grieved for my mother. It felt as though I lost her along with my brother. My first psychotherapist, a Freudian, spoke this to me. I eventually sensed it too.

Mother took the death very hard and experienced many emotional breakdowns. She picked up the Bible the first thing and clutched it with all her might. Rightfully so, God's word became her escape and comfort from the severe loss. In one way I loved her, but in another way I hated what she and the family were becoming. Before Jeff's death we used to have a picnic every Sunday with all the relatives and boyfriends. This vanished with Jeff.

Mother withdrew from society as a whole. She went to church every day. She would sing the high Catholic masses and give money to the church for Jeff's soul.

I did learn one thing from the teaching of the Catholic Church: reverence. This has served me well in my later years. I am finally learning to become more humble.

After several years of struggling with the Bible and the Catholic Church and its doctrines, my mother left the church. Ironically, the last time my mother went there was for my wedding with my wife Samantha. Mother and some of the Catholic members seemed to argue all the time about the Bible. It even got to the point where they dug Jeff's body up from the Catholic cemetery and moved him across the road to the Protestant cemetery. I dreamed I was pulling his casket up with a heavy rope one night. I was not told of the reburial till after the fact.

From there Mother evolved into the Charismatic Christianity Movement. I found a lot of their practices fake, from falsely speaking in tongues to being slain by the spirit and falling over. I believe that some practices were real and some were not. I also believe that tongues is not something you turn on but is turned on by the Holy Spirit at His beckoning, not yours. I could be wrong with my perception, but I believe not.

I also questioned a lot of their healing practices. The ministers would always heal something you couldn't see. Why couldn't they recover eyesight, restore a limb? Most all of them cured pains and arthritis. With my mother it was always who was right and who was wrong with religion. It was always black and white. Many times in my depression I would argue with her, "Take the board out of your eye first before you take the splinter from your neighbor's."

She became angry with me and would tell me in an accusing way that I knew it all. I withdrew from our arguments even more into a world of depression. Religion became very depressing for me, but I would in time return to the Bible.

*'Do not judge so that you will not be judged.
'For in the way you judge, you will be judged; and by your standards of measure it will be measured to you.
Why do you look at the speck that is in your brother's eye, but do not notice the log that is in your own eye?'*

Matthew 7:1–3

This verse has become a symbol for me to help me keep myself in check regarding the way I treat and speak to other people. This is a continuation of the Old Testament verse "an eye for an eye." I do believe that God does make things right in the long run.

Recovering the Best I Could

My first love was the game of basketball. I played it in all of my spare time. I was overweight but still was able to make the basketball team in junior high. I struggled in school those first two years after Jeff died. I cheated a lot in the seventh and eighth grade. This is how I kept my exam scores up in those years. I was so scared of failing. I became dishonest in my schoolwork. I had no social life except for church. I found some support when I visited my sisters, though. At home I lay around and fantasized in the darkness of my mind. Looking back I had a very stagnant life. Grief had overwhelmed me. There was so much darkness in the day. I wanted to socialize with girls and date. I was afraid of rejection, of being put down again. I felt inferior toward all women at that time and even later in my adult life.

As I graduated from the eighth grade into high school the classes got more difficult. I remember in my sophomore year having trouble in plane geometry. I was getting Ds. I studied and thought and studied more. I even was trying to solve problems in my sleep. Then all at once I understood the concepts. I got As after that. I then applied my problem-solving skills in other courses. Following this process I got high grades throughout high school and graduated fifth in my class.

The gift of problem solving helped me to graduate from college as an engineer with a 3.49 GPA in my later years. I relate this as a gift God gave me from his favor. It was not without a struggle, though, and a lot of perseverance. I still had problems with writing and English, though, and still do, but I am getting better.

My greatest gift was in basketball. Between my sophomore and junior year in high school I got a job in a tomato patch with a local farmer. He had thirty-four thousand tomatoes to care for. We were hired to hoe, tie, and finally pick the tomatoes. He hired four people to do the work. My best friend and I were among them. I knelt in the patch caring for the tomatoes eight hours a day. I lost weight and became very strong and thin. At the beginning of my junior year in basketball, I went from the slowest man on the team to the fastest in one year. I just kept running and running and running.

For to one is given the word of wisdom through the Spirit, and to another the word of knowledge according the same Spirit.

1 Corinthians 12:8

I believe that God gave me the gift of solving problems in school through hard studying. I also believe that this gift became a stumbling block when I was dealing with my emotional mental condition. I was always trying to fix me, reading books on psychology and self-help books. I became like a hypochondriac with mental illness.

Victories and Defeats

I struggled in high school socially and mentally but was determined to work my way through. I continued to serve mass every day at the Catholic Church while I attended Milford High School. I began to excel at my schoolwork even more. I had renewed strength in basketball due to the summer tomato patch work, which was now paying off. I did have a setback in basketball, though. Before the season started I broke my shooting wrist playing around with weights at the house of one of my friends. I had one beer, and it proved too much. I paid the consequences by sitting out the first half of the junior-year basketball season and had to shoot left-handed. I was a right-handed shooter. My senior year proved better for grades and also in basketball. I also had my first class appointment as the senior president.

I had recaptured my self-esteem by succeeding with these events. I was riding high, but it took a lot of hard work. My motivation came from somewhere within. My mother and father did not attend any of my school events, including basketball where I finally made co-captain during my senior year.

CHAPTER 4
1970–1977

For this reason a man shall leave his father and mother, and be joined to his wife; and they shall become one flesh.

GENESIS 2:24

I do believe that when I married my first wife Samantha I did become one with her. After she divorced me I only felt like half a person. I had no one to talk to on an emotional level. I think at this point I internalized and talked to myself a lot. Inside the voices would never stop. I just did a lot of arguing back and forth in my mind. The divorce with her initiated the second emotional breakdown in my life.

Dating

I met my first date in a vegetable garden working for her dad. Pamela was a beautiful young girl and a hard worker. She was in the eighth grade, and I was a junior in high school. She reminded me of an Indian princess with her long black hair. One day when we were alone at her dad's lake we kissed. It was the first time I kissed a girl. Sometime later I took her to some local football games. My friend Mike began dating her older sister, and this is how we had to go out together, as a double date. Since Pamela was in the eighth grade I got a lot of static from my friends. They called me a cradle robber, and more cruel words came from my peers.

I met my next date after I had played an outstanding basketball game. Our team at Milford beat a team ranked tenth in the state. After the game my friend and I took Samantha and Candy to my place. Samantha was in my class, so the cradle-robbing comments stopped. I dropped Pamela for Samantha and over the years regretted the way I handled that. Pamela later punched me in the arm at a school dance while I was with Samantha. I deserved much more for being so inconsiderate to Pamela.

On New Year's Eve in 1970 I took out my second date, Samantha. It was seven years after Jeff died. Seven years became a significant number in my trials. Every seven years something significant seemed to happen in my life.

Samantha was a beautiful girl, another long-, dark-haired Indian princess. She was in my class, so the harassment from my friends finally stopped. It was replaced with some jealousy since she could pass as a model. She also was smart, tops in the class. She worked hard also. Samantha and I continued seeing each other and finally became committed to each other. We went to the movies a lot. We never did know what was on. We were always making out in the back seat. This was like an elixir for me since I did not have closure with Jeff when I slept with him. It became a narcotic with my emotions. I could not get enough holding and touching. Samantha was good at making out. We steamed up many windows.

I was very mischievous then and riding high on my ego. As an older teenager I thought I knew it all. I began drinking some; this was socially accepted in Samantha's family but not in mine. Samantha's family had to deal with alcoholism, especially with their father. I always liked to hear him tell the story of my grandfather and him gigging fish in the river. He must have told me this story a hundred times.

After graduating from high school Samantha and I went off to separate colleges about fifty miles apart. I went to PSU, and she went to College Tech. As a relationship goes we inevitably lost our virginity. This became an elixir for both of us. We could not stand to be apart. We quit school after one semester. We came home and worked. I drove a truck for my father and Uncle Sam. Samantha became a waitress. The following year we both commuted to a local community college in Milford, Ohio. We went there for two years, and Samantha graduated as a registered nurse. I got two years of college in for a four-year engineering degree. We then planned to get married on June 28, 1973.

For our struggle is not against flesh and blood, but against rulers, against the powers, against the world forces of the darkness …

EPHESIANS 6:12

I do believe that the evil that people do is indirectly in our makeup. It is handed down through generations in families, almost like a curse. This can come in almost all cases in verbal and physical abuse. In therapy you try to break the handing down of the curse and heal yourself. I believe no one is immune.

WRESTLING WITH **G**OD

In April of 1973 my future wife and I, in response to a request from my family, went to a Catholic retreat called a Cursillo. Samantha went first. It lasted for three days. I noticed a change in her on her return. It was then my turn. The retreat lasted over a weekend. There were a series of talks about Christ and His church. One of the speakers was a priest. He gave a talk on the suffering and death of Christ on the cross. He talked of how Christ struggled to breathe while suffering on the cross. The talk moved me tremendously. I began to feel guilty for my sexual relationship with Samantha.

The first night I went to sleep on a cot. In my dreams I remember being twisted as you twist a towel. I had water squeezed out of me as I slept. The next morning I awoke in sheets soaked with sweat. I sensed that in this dream God and Satan were battling for my soul. God was twisting from one end and Satan the other. I was a towel in between with water being squeezed out of me.

Sometime after this I confessed to a priest about my sexual behavior. I cried heavily and was relieved. I could barely get the words out as I confessed to the priest. As the Cursillo concluded we were told to get up in front of the church congregation and tell of our experiences. I recall saying that it is different out in the world than it is in here.

The Cursillo concluded, and my mom and dad and Samantha came to pick me up. As we drove home I recall feeling so loved by God and thankful for my family. I felt one with God. When I got home they helped me to bed because I was so high and drunk on God. I never again have felt the love from God as I did that night. In the following days I would sing and drive my truck. I was happy again. Some denominations call this the Baptism of the Holy Spirit and being filled with new wine. I would agree. I actually felt drunk at times, although I did not consume any alcohol.

I was not able to keep my commitment to God and Samantha as I should in the next few months. This is the world of my flesh I was talking about at the Cursillo concluding speech. Samantha and I were married in June with a charismatic-type Catholic mass. The service was very moving, with guitar-accompanied singing. At the reception we served wine only. My in-laws were upset that I didn't serve other alcoholic beverages, and my mother was not happy with the wine. I thought wine and a wedding feast were quite appropriate at a Christian wedding at the time. This was my mother's last time attending the Catholic Church. She was excommunicated for refusing to call the priest "father," she told me.

*'Do not call anyone on earth your father; for
One is your Father, He who is in Heaven.'*

MATTHEW 23:9

My mother took this verse literally. Should you not call your earthly father, "father"? I think a lot of people taking verses out of context actually cause themselves a lot of grief, including me …

Our Marriage

After our short honeymoon I went to work driving with my uncle Sam in an eighteen-wheeler across the eastern part of the country. Samantha acted strange on our honeymoon, I think my reluctance to remain sexually inactive till the wedding caused her grief and hurt our relationship. She was not one to talk about these things; she remained quiet and I just sensed them.

I was elated with the traveling involved with being a truck driver but missed Samantha. She stayed in Milford and worked as a registered nurse at PSU. I missed her while traveling and later regretted that I didn't call her enough. After two years on the road with my uncle, I began driving by myself. This was somewhat frightening, but I managed. In 1975 my truck driving ended with a layoff from the truck-driving company. I then went to work with my wife's oldest brother building industrial bins.

Samantha and I then purchased our first home, which was a few years old. We had also purchased a new car a year earlier. We had seen our financial dreams coming true. I went again on the road from the East Coast to the West with this job. I saw Samantha intermittently on weekends and time off from my job. The work was very hard, with long hours and lots of traveling time.

In the summer of 1976 I noticed my wife distancing from me. I wondered why. She got a staph infection in her finger one day and was hospitalized for a few days. I left work on the road and came back home to see her. Samantha was very standoffish that I had come back when I went to visit her in the hospital. At this time I think Samantha was having an affair with a doctor. She wrote John Denver lyrics at home and seemed elated over something other than myself. She became cold with me and distanced herself. I became angry because of this and yelled at her. At one point that summer I sent her back home to her parents. In time I asked her to come back. I was very angry and unhappy and confused and lonely.

For a righteous man falls seven times, and rise again.

Proverbs 24:16

I now had fallen emotionally twice. None was my doing. Was this my lot in life? This verse gave me comfort in knowing of the possibility of another beginning.

My First Divorce

In 1976 on New Year's Eve at around 6:00 pm I was playing pool in the basement of the house we had bought. Samantha came down the basement steps and sat down on them. "I have something to tell you," she said.

"What?" I asked.

"I'm seeing someone …"

"Who?"

"The pharmacist at the hospital."

I immediately threw the pool stick at the wall and it shattered. My anger frightened me. This was to the hour seven years since I took her out on our first date. Later I learned that her lover was a doctor who had taken her flying in his plane. He had a wife and children. I was immediately overwhelmed with anger and told her to leave. I actually left and went to a house of ill repute. I cried all the way. I was so alone inside and out.

The next day I fell to my knees in the backyard and grieved heavily. I did not know what to do. I was overwhelmed with grief. I was broken again. I had sensations in bed while I was sleeping that my body was very big, and I felt an overwhelming sense of emotions prior to Samantha's confession. I believe that this was a gauge of my emotional level. I was trying to hold back the dam of my emotions.

Be anxious for nothing, but in everything by prayer and supplication with thanksgiving let your request be made known to God.

PHILIPPIANS 4:6

This verse has been my salvation in anxious moments. I have memorized this verse since 1992. It needs no explanation. I wish I knew of it sooner.

The First Year Alone

I had asked my first wife if she wanted to try therapy to maybe help our situation. I sensed that throughout our relationship she felt that I was the one who was messed up because of my brother's death that no one, including me, ever spoke of. Consequently, she did not need therapy; I did. I believe she was right, but it did not justify her actions. Many years later, in life after the divorce, I mentioned our relationship. She said that we were just children then. I think that again she rationalized her guilt away and did not take responsibility for her actions. Why is it that people who need therapy are the crazy ones? Or are they just the injured ones?

I begged Samantha to stay. I still loved her. She did not want therapy. She told me that she would think about whether to get a divorce or not. She had control of the marriage this way. At this time in history the women's liberation movement was at a high, and I felt that this influenced her. She wanted to be free.

She wanted me to go back to work on the road with her brother to a job in Florida. I refused the job because the work area was fifty-plus feet in the air. Why should I risk my life in Florida while she messed around back at home? I concluded that I would go to see my sister Eudora in California to get away and think. Through this trial I kept having the feeling of doing something quick; let me fix it quick. I also felt down over what Samantha said to me, and it wasn't even my fault. I think this was due to my PTSD over Jeff's accident or to whatever disorder I was suffering from. Words that people spoke to me literally picked me up or put me down; whether it was true or not, it didn't matter to me at this time. They were just haunting words. I think that if I had developed some communication skills after Jeff died I would be a better communicator with my emotions.

Samantha drove me to the airport in Milford, Ohio, and the whole trip was very quiet and sad for me. I was "Leaving on a Jet Plane" by listening to the Mamas and Papas song, which was a hit at this time. I was broken again. I finally arrived in California to a scene of hippies and so-called freedom. I walked, ran, and thought and thought and thought. I had visions of another man making love to Samantha. This vision was driving me insane. I had become sexually isolated from my wife and emotionally confused.

After a week of soul searching I decided to go home and face my demons. In retrospect I should have stayed away and tried to start a new life but did not know how. My social and survival skills were terrible. I did not know what to do.

I flew back after a week and went to Mom and Dad's home; another mistake. I missed my parents and family but had become distant from my years working on the road. I came home as the prodigal son.

I was emotionally strung out and couldn't think of a solution. I decided to go back to Samantha's and my home. As I approached the house I noticed a Mercedes Benz in my garage. I was shaking with anger and fear. I knocked on the door, and Samantha opened it and asked me what I was doing here. I don't know why I just didn't walk in. I wanted to shoot the guy.

I shook with fear, a mixture of hate and fear. She spoke harshly to me, as if I had done something wrong, "What are you doing here?"

This point instigated my breakdown. She had the power of persuasion over me even when she was wrong. Somewhere in my life I held women in my family and outside my family as being better than I. It has shown up as an inferiority complex within me. Four older sisters at home in my youth did not help. I left but wanted to trash the Mercedes with a sledge hammer. I regret over the years that I did not do this.

CHAPTER 5
1977–1984

You know my reproach my shame and my dishonor;
All my adversaries are before You.

P<small>SALM</small> 69:19

After separating from Samantha I was totally ashamed. My closest relative spoke harshly to me. My father slammed the Bible down in my room and told me if I had read it this never would have happened. So now I had verbally taken the blame for Jeff's death and Samantha's infidelity. It seemed like life was backward for me. What should be was not. What was should not have been.

Fully Ashamed

I tried to hide in sleep at my parent's house but ended up wanting to die.

I truly wanted to die but was scared of dying at the same time. At this point the fear of death probably saved my life. I recall holding a gun to my head several times after the divorce and contemplating suicide. I found a gun in the glove box of my truck. To this day I am not sure who put it there.

As I lay in bed one night I felt my body start to rise above the bed. It made me very full of anxiety. I became frightened to die … but I wanted to die. I was a mess.

I finally tried to go back to work with the company that I was working for building industrial silos. I could barely function. I was extremely depressed. I could not function or think well. I had no good energy. My world had collapsed around me. I was heavy with depression and in shock. At this point I was much lower physically than I was at Jeff's death.

I quit my job with the company and went back to Mom and Dad's to recuperate as the prodigal son. I needed a friend but found no one. I was back with the dysfunctional family from Jeff's death. I had nowhere to lay my head, as the Bible would say; another verse I related to Christ.

At this time Mom and Dad were attending a very conservative fundamentalist church. The religious rhetoric was thick, as was my depression. They lived and breathed words from their minister. They watched him on TV every evening. This guy knew all, according to my parents. He was the answer and the answers to my problems. The overall problem that I had was my sinning, according to the religious folk. This caused my depressive state. This was the noncommunicative impression I got from my mom and dad and some of my siblings.

I then went to see a doctor for help. He gave me some antidepressants. Taking medicine for depression or anxiety was also wrong, according to my family at this time. Later in life my family changed their minds about psychotic medicine, since some of them came to be on it in some form or another.

I was totally hopeless and had nowhere to turn. I remember smoking a cigarette in the bathroom of the fundamentalist church one Sunday. A minister came in and smelled smoke and started beating on the toilet door and told me to get out. In retrospect, I should have said I'm covering up the smell; the smell of religion, that is.

I sat there and flushed the cigarette down the toilet and waited. Finally he left, full of himself. At one point one of my sisters wanted me go to a Bible-study class there too. I reluctantly decided to try again. I sat down in a chair in one of the church's rooms. I looked up to see seven unsaved people's names on the board. My name was the seventh. The minister came in and in front of everyone told me that this Bible study would not help me. I sat quietly and waited for this class to end. I left with thoughts of never returning to that church again. And so it was.

And He said to them, 'Rightly did Isaiah prophesy of you hypocrites, as it is written:

*"THIS PEOPLE HONORS ME WITH THEIR LIPS,
BUT THEIR HEART IS FAR AWAY FROM ME.
BUT IN VAIN THEY DO WORSHIP ME,
TEACHING THE DOCTRINES OF THE PRECEPTS OF MEN."
'Neglecting the commandment of God,
you hold to the tradition of men.'*

MARK 7:6–8

I think that God, Christ, and the Holy Spirit have some issues with religious people. I had issues with religious people, including those in my family. Religious Jewish leaders crucified Christ. I also at time felt as if I was being crucified mentally.

Mental Asylum Admission

I went to work for my brother-in-law building houses to try to pay for my keep with my parents. He had married one of my older twin sisters before Jeff died. Their marriage was on the rocks because my sister had left the Catholic Church. Consequently, when my mom left she took most of the family with her. My brother-in-law was a devout Catholic and did not budge when it came to Catholicism. While I was working with him he told me about all of the issues between my sister and him. He was very angry, and I became his sounding board for his anger and frustration. His words hurt me terribly, because I loved everyone, I thought. I was slowly changing my views of my family.

After Jeff's death I became very sensitive to my family members' relationships with one another. This was due to Jeff and me fighting at times. Then Jeff died, and I could not handle the thought of separation. One of my sisters and her boyfriend broke up, and it devastated me, I think more than they. I moved out of Mom and Dad's home again and into an apartment in Milford. I had to get out and away. I lived in the basement of a retired older lady. She was very nice and had two sons who were ministers. I just couldn't get away from religious people.

I recall during most of this period being unable to relax and focus on anything. I always had a running mind and a hypersensitive body going at a very fast rate. I fantasized about being with Samantha at times and felt spiritually close but yet so far away. I had heard through her relatives that she had moved to Chapel Hill, North Carolina. A vision that I kept in my head was of ten years passing and then me being mentally normal again. I had no way of knowing how to do this, though.

I tried to recover on my own and read self-help books. I became very paranoid. I felt like people were talking about me all the time. After Jeff died people talked about me in my presence, like I didn't exist. I was very hyper physically. I ran ten miles one day without any practicing. My mind was so jumbled that I couldn't read a paragraph without other thoughts evading. After giving myself one year, I decided to see a psychiatrist. This was even after I tried a doctor who put me on a lot of vitamins and a protein diet. That did not work either. I went to the psychiatrist and told him of my shaking, twitching, and having no ability to concentrate. He guessed and gave me the drug Navane and said, "I doubt if it will help."

Here we go again, words that kill … I left even more discouraged than when I came in. At this same doctor's office I made an appointment with my first therapist. I wanted to talk about Jeff and felt that I should and needed to. This discussion about Jeff's death was long overdue. If my family had sat down after Jeff died and asked us all to talk about it this would have saved me from being acquainted with grief for so long and so late in life!

My first visit to the therapist included me trying to talk about Jeff and my past. Deep down I felt it was wrong to talk about Jeff, but I continued to talk. I did get out some sentences and tried to piece together my past. There was so much emotion behind my memory of Jeff's accident that I did not know how to handle it. My rational thinking became nonexistent at this time. The therapist's comment to me was to "stop rationalizing."

I did not understand. He kept telling me from our talks that I was looking for my mother. Later I believed he was right. I lost her to depression after Jeff died. I also became afraid of my emotions because of their intensity.

Weeks went by, and I continued to work building houses with my brother-in-law. Everyone said to stay busy. After a year I gave up running and settled into a heavy depressive state on Navane. I then asked the therapist to admit me to a mental hospital in Milford, Ohio. I decided to become friends with insanity. It seemed at the time that if my world wasn't sane maybe a mental hospital would be.

I am guiltless;
I do not take notice of myself;
I despise my life.

JOB 9:21

I am guiltless. I do not take notice of myself. I despise my life.

SHAWN

First Series of Shock Treatments

I entered the hospital feeling very scared and hoping that something or someone would help me there. There were all types of people there, even people who committed crimes and people who wanted to kill themselves. Many people had tried suicide. I recall lying in my bed and shaking and wanting some relief through sleep.

I stood in line to see my therapist along with other patients. He would pinch the skin on my hand to see if I was dehydrated. When I entered the hospital, I was on a drug called Navane. From there he tried me on Triavil and lithium carbonate. I didn't respond to his liking. I was under the gun of having only three weeks to recover while my insurance would cover the cost of hospitalization. Consequently, within a week they told me they wanted to give me ECTs, or shock treatments. I felt like I had been given the death penalty. I called my sister Eudora. She was scared for me, as was I. I reluctantly signed their release forms, and the ECTs were scheduled.

I was not allowed to eat after nine o'clock at night in an effort to prevent me from choking during the treatment. Early one morning, since I lost track of time and didn't know what day it was, I was taken upstairs in a long white robe. They laid me on a bed. Next to me was a device like a headset with paddles on it. The nurse said they would give me an injection that would paralyze me. They said I would go to sleep and stop breathing and they would manually breathe for me with an air bag. As they gave me the injection I remember feeling the drug run up my arm. It reached my brain with a cool feeling, and a loud buzzing sound engulfed my brain. After that I remember nothing.

I had a series of three shock treatments and have very little memory of them. The only memory I have is of walking between my bed and the ECT room. I awoke one morning a week or so later. Mom and Dad were standing next to my bed. My legs were still twitching a little, but the high anxiety with racing thoughts was gone. I was pleased to see them. They said very little of the situation, just light talk. That night I got up and went to the lounge. I looked out over the city of Milford with all the lights. The lights were beautiful … just like my childhood when we would watch the Christmas tree lights. I was at peace with everything. I enjoyed drinking soda as if it were the first time I tasted the drink. I played my guitar and sang Simon and Garfunkel songs. I played for all the patients and was at peace. Looking back, a lot of the feelings I had were from prior to Jeff's accident. They were good and homey and very peaceful.

I met a female patient in the hospital, and we became friends. She was married but said she was getting a divorce. We both obtained leave from the psych unit and left the hospital together one day. We ran around and stayed at my apartment for one night.

I was then discharged in the allotted time for my insurance to cover my expenses. Our discharges occurred within days of one another. She gradually was recovering from a childhood abuse that caused her to forget parts of the present. All was bliss for a while till her husband came for her at her sister's house while I was visiting her. I politely left. I then again retreated to my folks' house as a repetitive prodigal son. I was also broke spiritually and financially again. The problem with the prodigal son was that the fatted calf was never roasted for the party and there was no party, just my return home from sinning. This cycle kept repeating itself.

After the hospital stay the doctors had me on lithium carbonate and Triavil. I lay around a lot like after Jeff died. I became anxious and unhappy again with no visions of the future, just being and then dying. After some months and some deliberation I decided to come off my medication. Of course I was not the prodigal son, so I quit taking my medicine to try and break the curse. Those who needed medication were not right with God. This is how my family made me feel. I wish at that time we could have sat down and talked about what happened with Jeff.

There were some positive emotions as I came off of the medicine, but in about seven days I hit bottom. One evening I was over at my sister Penny's house, sitting in front of her. I was very angry. I wanted to say something but did not know what. This is the same sister whom I was yelling at to help Jeff when he was on fire.

I could not speak. I finally froze and became catatonic in front of Penny. I remember being conscious in my mind but could not move a muscle. I thought I died but was still conscious inside of my body. I could think somewhat, but I could not move a muscle. My father and brother-in-law picked me up and loaded me into a car. Penny then drove me to the doctor. The doctor who was with Jeff when he died gave me an injection. They asked me, "How could you do this to yourself?"

My response should have been, who is doing what to whom? They carried me back home to bed, and I slept all night. At one time one of the local doctors at that office told me I should just get drunk.

*'Oh that You would hide me in Sheol,
That You would conceal me untill Your wrath returns to You,
That You would set a limit for me and remember me!
'If a man dies, will he live again?
All the days of my struggle I will wait
Until my change comes."*

Job 14:13–14

I could relate to a lot of verses from Job. I did not like to live in these verses, though. They were very sad and lonely and depressive.

Second Series of Shock Treatments

The next morning I awoke extremely low, and my face was drawn downward. I later thought that I had Bell's palsy. I tried to walk it off but couldn't. I asked my sister Jane to take me to the mental hospital at Milford. For some reason I could not get my family to help me with these decisions to get medical help. Religious help was always given, though, free of charge.

I arrived and was examined by the doctor who gave me the shock treatments. He sat me on the exam table and checked my reflexes. I had none, and I asked why this was. He said because I was depressed. I then went back to a room.

They put me on some medicine that was unknown to me. I recall the following night talking to a nurse on the night shift as she watched over me. She said I should be a doctor. The next morning I awoke in an emotional state, split apart from the previous night's discussion with the nurse. I recollected none of the discussion. I just had a vague memory of talking all night. I awoke emotionally conscious walking through the dining room the next morning. A security guard was beside me. I think I split for the first time that night between rational and emotional thought. The emotion was the same as my childhood awareness. The rational part of my mind was the one I was developing. I believe that the rational part is the one I talked with to the nurse that night. I am sure the drugs they gave me enhanced the splitting.

They then told me they were going to give me more shock treatments. I waited a few days for my next series of treatments, and then they tried three more. During the third one they had difficulty getting me to breathe again, so they quit giving them to me. They said I almost died. I was extremely low and full of anxiety after all of this, and my thoughts raced like the wind and were disassociated. I remember very little, including at one point not knowing who I was. Still, though, I knew of God.

While I was in my hospital room they put an older man named Roy in the room next to me. He became extremely loud and destructive and even tore the sink off the wall. This went on for days. They thought he would die because his blood pressure went very high. I was told they were giving him the drug Haladol to calm him. He cussed and shouted and yelled at President Truman for the war efforts. I was also told he was a Sunday school teacher. Now wasn't that a coincidence.

I became very paranoid and thought Satan was after me through Roy. I wore out a pair of tennis shoes by just walking the halls on a new medicine, Serentil. I remember meeting Roy in the hall one day and putting my hands on him. My sister and nephew happened to come off the elevator at the same time and witnessed my actions. Roy spoke, "Help me," and I then let go. After that the staff became very hostile toward me and kept moving me from room to room. At one point I refused to move; I was very confused. Four nurses came in my room and gave me a shot in each arm and then dragged me to another room. I did not resist. I then became very low.

All Your commandments are faithful;
They have persecuted me with a lie; Help Me!
They almost destroyed me on earth,
But as for me, I do not forsake Your precepts.
Revive me according to Your loving kindness,
So that I may keep the testimony of Your mouth.

PSALMS 119:86–88

I remember thinking through these trials to hold on for forty days, which comes from scripture. I would walk and walk and walk and walk and then wait for the forty days to be up. I seemed to never make it to forty days, though. Relief always came early.

Jean and College

While I was at the mental hospital I met Jean, a nurse's aid, whom they assigned to watch me. We became very friendly to each other, and visions of being with Jean gave me an incentive to recover. At one point I got a grounds pass. I thought it meant I could go to her house by way of ground. This was wrong, and I offended the head psychiatrist. I was then confined to the unit. Eventually I recuperated enough that I went home to Mom and Dad's again, and again the prodigal son returned. Of course I was broke again. I never seemed to get out of this cycle …

This stay only lasted a short time. My therapist then applied for me to get Social Security benefits. I moved out from Mom and Dad's with about two hundred dollars to my name. I rented a small apartment and waited but again became very low. I tried a job in the oilfields of southern Ohio but could not hold it down. I applied for and received food stamps. Finally a Social Security check came in the mail and I was able to upgrade my living environment and move to a better apartment. I then had thoughts of going back to school and moved into a larger apartment with Jean, my live-in nurse's aide. I put my efforts back to obtaining a degree in engineering. Again I practiced my problem-solving skills at Milford College.

Jean continued to work at the hospital. One evening she went to a staff party and I went with her. My therapist came in and gave me the finger. I never went to him again. I eventually even weaned myself off the medication Serentil.

The Spirit and the bride say, 'Come!' And let him who hears say, 'Come.' And let the one who is thirsty; come; Let the one who wishes take the water of life without cost.

REVELATION 22:17

My belief in the Holy Spirit has allowed her to show up at times. I am grateful to God for her.

My Second Therapist

I continued with my studies in school. While attending Milford College and living with Jean, I still found myself struggling with depression and sadness and even started hearing cracking noises in my head. I was still able to stay off medication, though. I finally went to see a therapist in Milford at a local mental health office. I waited a few weeks and then finally got in to see her. She was a Gestalt-trained therapist. She had one bad habit, though: she smoked a lot, as I did. This gave me hope that she could help me.

I was able to relate my past to her, and she was very empathetic. She once said I should be sitting behind her desk and not her. During one deep discussion I became very uneasy. I unconsciously split and turned my chair to the left and looked up at the corner of the wall in her office and said, "I am the bride of Christ."

She tried to always coach me too in listening to myself. She also said that the cracking noise in my head at night was my anger.

Tremble, and do not sin;
Mediate in your heart on your bed, and be still.

Psalm 4:4

Does God say to be angry here … just don't sin …?

Breaking Up and PSU Hospital

Jean also became a part-time student at Milford College while she worked at the hospital. I attended full-time. We had some good times talking about psychotherapy, which was her field of study. While she continued to work at the mental hospital, one of the patients was jumping out from behind doors at her, which made her very nervous. She also related to me a story about her holding a knife to someone's throat in the past. She was an atheist and thought that when you die everything goes black. I had trouble with her belief. After one year I wanted to end the relationship but did not have the courage to do so. She picked up on my feelings, though, and dropped me.

The ongoing power struggle with the women I was with remained. Mother was the first in dominating my life. I did not realize the impact that Jean had on me till she was gone. The feelings of abandonment hit me hard again. I started walking and walking and walking. As I lay down one morning after being up all night, my body doubled up and said, "Help me."

I split between body and mind. The words "help me" keep taking on more meaning for me, from trying to scream help for Jeff to mental hospital splits. I became haunted by the words. Also at the mental hospital the insane Roy said this to me …

I was alone again. I drove myself into the ground worrying about all kinds of psychological talk from my therapy. I thought my therapist regressed me back to my childhood and was angry at her for doing this if she did. I do believe I had regressed with the first series of shock treatments though.

As I tried to sleep one night I had a vivid dream of a snake biting me on my back. The next morning I developed a rash there and consequently went to the local emergency room. They said I was bitten by an animal. They gave me cortisone. Could this be psychosomatic? I wonder what the snake meant—Satan or sex? I then continued to struggle with walking constantly with no sleep, just thinking. I couldn't stop walking. I was awake for several days and could not rest.

At one point I was remembering my Cursillo days. I was sitting at my table in the apartment, and my neighbor Dave came over. I recall feeling as if the Holy Spirit had filled me up to the brink; I was feeling Christ's suffering. My neighbor Dave was sitting at the table in the kitchen. He started to sway like he was drunk. Some candy wrapped in cellophane in the dish on the table started moving and crackling. Dave left and then kept coming back in for more spiritual wine. He wanted to know what was going on, and I told him it was the Holy Spirit. He finally left and went back to his apartment, intoxicated.

The next day I kept walking and couldn't stop. I called Eudora in Washington DC. She said she would come to my place immediately. When she got there she saw my exhaustion with the mental fight inside of me. As I came in from a walk my sister arrived. I heard a voice in my head say, "Hi."

I sat on the floor in front of the door exhausted and afraid in front of Eudora. The next morning she took me to Milford Hospital to see if I could get something to help me rest. I was feeling low in my chest clear down to my belly. I was going mad inside. I kept thinking I wanted to die just like Jeff. They gave me a shot, and I went back to the apartment with Eudora and finally rested.

That same day I went to see my therapist with Eudora. The therapist said I set her up since my sister was there. Bringing Eudora upset her. I then asked her if she would quit smoking with me through this experience. She got even more upset. I agreed to be admitted to Grant Hall at PSU. My therapist told me I would have to work hard. I felt like I needed a vacation; in a way this was a very expensive vacation.

On my return to her office at one point we went to a different room. I looked into the adjacent room and saw that there were cameras pointing through holes in the wall. I spoke harshly of this and the fact that I was being filmed without my permission. She looked ashamed. I left then and never returned.

I dropped out of school and went to the mental hospital at Grant Hall. I remember having mood swings, from being elated at times to being paranoid and feeling low. They initially locked me up on the ward. My chest hurt tremendously because of all the anxiety. One morning I felt as if they were going to lock me up forever. I decided to kill myself. The only thing sharp I could find was a paper clip. I went into my room and started digging away at my wrist. Soon two students came in with a Bible and caught me. They said, "What are you thinking?"

I told them I was Christ and I was being persecuted. My thinking was very confused with who and what I was. I felt as if people wanted me to disappear.

The doctors then gave me Triliphon, and I walked and walked and walked. I then settled down with some good nights of sleep and, after three weeks, was discharged.

For the word of God is living and active and sharper than any two-edged sword, piercing as far as the division of soul and spirit, of both joints and marrow, and able to judge the thoughts and intentions of the heart.

Hebrews 4:12

I believe that my soul was split from my body at times. I believe that this was due to the inner battle inside of me, soul … body … mind or soul … God … Satan. I continually accept that the Holy Spirit resides in me and corrects me.

First Out-of-Body Experience

After getting out of the hospital in May of 1980 I was proud to get a scholarship from Amazon Oil Company in Decatur, Illinois, and left for a summer intern job there. I made arrangements with another student to room with me in a trailer. It was on one of these nights in the trailer while I was sleeping that I found myself out of my body. I was floating down the hallway of the trailer bouncing face down off the floor. The hallway was lit up, but no lights were on. I became conscious that I was out of my body and became extremely scared. I awoke back in my bed on my back. This was more than a dream and was very frightening at the time.

I continued to work and had one visit from Jean in mid-summer. She wanted a commitment from me to get married, but I did not give her one. It disturbed me that she was an atheist. This should not have bothered me, because she was kinder than most of my relatives.

But he himself went a days journey into the wilderness, and came and sat down under a juniper tree; and he requested for himself that he might die, and said, 'It is enough; now, O Lord, take my life, for I am not better than my fathers.'

1 Kings 19:4

At this point in my depression I really became serious about suicide with no fear ...

Suicide

I came back to Milford, Ohio, from working with Amazon Oil Company in Illinois in the fall of 1980. I asked mom and dad if I could live with them to finish college. They agreed again. I only had about two thousand dollars and could only squeak by to finish college. I felt like this was a homecoming initially for me. Again depression was in the air after I was there for a few weeks.

I took a local girl out and had a good time watching fireworks in Milford, but when I asked her out again she gave me excuses. I felt as if she knew of my past with mental illness and did not want to be involved. The local gossip in a small town was always evident. I felt abandoned again. I remember the loneliness starting to come in as I sat next to the small shed in Mom and Dad's yard. I looked to God and felt nothing. I decided to take my life.

I went to the basement of Mom and Dad's house where I set up a temporary office for schoolwork. I found the first thing I could get my hands on, an arrow from my bow. It had razor blades on it. I took the arrow and slashed my wrist. I lay down on the couch and waited for sleep, which was always a comfort to me. It didn't work; I kept clotting off. I then became frustrated and went up on the porch bleeding. Father saw me and asked me, "What are you trying to do, kill your mother?"

I said nothing again. Mother saw me and ran one hundred yards from the house to get Penny. She then fainted on her way back and passed out in the yard. They called an emergency squad for me. They came and bandaged me up and took me to Milford Hospital. Mom also ended up in the hospital with high blood pressure. I convinced them to take me to PSU, since they had no idea what to do with a suicidal patient at Milford. I had to make all these decision about myself. No one in my family helped me with the responsibility of trying to get well. They would offer only religious rhetoric.

They kept me locked up for one week while putting me on another antidepressant. I felt bad for Mom with shame and guilt for making her blood pressure rise, but in no way was I trying to kill her. I believe it was me I was trying to kill. Was I missing something here? Was I always being blamed for something I wasn't responsible for? I was in shock for what people said to me. I was blamed again for something I did not do. I did not play with fire with Jeff! I was nowhere near the accident! My parents should have put up their gasoline and barrel burners. Also, did not Samantha choose the divorce? I chose to kill myself. If it wasn't for my insecurity of being alone I should have left the area forever … despair became a horrible feeling.

I carried my depression back to an apartment in Milford to get away and went back to see my therapist, who was always trying to get me to become one with my emotions. I became concerned about finishing Milford College with no money.

I became very depressed, and my therapist decided that I would go to a state medical hospital to get myself together, again. At least she was helping me to make a decision about myself.

I asked my uncle Larry to drive me there, and I was then admitted. The doctor there decided to take me off all medicine, which was Triliphon and the antidepressant they gave me at PSU. In about one week I hit bottom. My face drew downward, and I became very low and depressed.

My family decided to send two Christian girls to see me and invite me to the church where I was labeled as unsaved. I decided to try again; I would quit smoking as an act of faith, I thought. I made it till the following morning but eventually broke down and went to get a pack of cigarettes down the street. As I was very, very low in spirit, I uncontrollably stopped on the sidewalk, turned to the left, raised my head up, and said, "Banker."

I immediately turned to the right and felt even lower. I was broken and could not be fixed, I thought. In my thoughts I cried for help, but no one was there. I continued to go after my cigarettes and then went back to the hospital for help. As I made it back to the hospital I immediately went back to the ward and saw the doctor in his office. I told him what happened, and then he asked why I said "banker."

I didn't know. He said that if I had money I wouldn't be there. I left his office and planned my death again. He could have been right. The money and success I have now has helped me to be more secure.

I went to my room and found my razor, took out the blades, and headed out of the hospital to do myself in. I went up a short utility road and knelt down. I felt empty, depressed, and totally hopeless to help myself. I did not know what to say to a God who was not helping me. I thought that God had abandoned me as everyone else did. In retrospect I know He didn't, though.

I started to slice my left wrist. I cut it so deep that my thumb and first two fingers went numb from slicing the nerve on my left hand. It is still numb to this day and is a reminder of the lowliness of my being at that time. I again quit bleeding and then became angry and walked with my bleeding wrist past the hospital to a bridge located down the street. I went to the middle of the bridge and wanted to meet God. I was demanding it. I closed my eyes and dove off.

There was about a foot of water in the small river, and I landed in a horizontal position on my back. The impact snapped the watch off my wrist, and I lost one shoe. I felt as if my flesh was loosed from my bones. I cannot describe in words the force of falling around forty feet into a foot of water and landing flat on my back. I think if I had landed any other way I would have died. Maybe Jeff rotated me a little.

I remained conscious throughout the whole episode and finally just lay there in the water. There was no one to come to my rescue. After a few minutes in utter shock I then decided to go back to the hospital. I walked across the shallow river and up the river bank, struggling to keep my footing. I felt that I was walking crooked and that I was misaligned. As I walked into the ward the staff and patients came running to me. I went to my room and lay down on my bed. I was a mess. They called a squad, who took me back across the river to a local hospital. They x-rayed me and then stitched up my wrist. They said my back was broken, and they put me to bed in an extensive care unit. I remember that as I tried to sleep that night my back would spasm. I screamed and screamed throughout the night.

Early the next morning a young nurse came in my room and shaved me. She was very pretty. I was on pain medication, which was almost like a small taste of heaven. Later that day my uncle Larry visited me and asked me, "How could you do this to your family?"

I was speechless again. My cousin and his wife also showed up and asked me if I had anything to say.

*"What is my strength, that I should wait?
And what is my end, that I should endure?*

Job 6:11

I was pretty much a mess mentally, emotionally, and spiritually after the jump off the bridge. I was ready to meet God. He did not want to meet me then. Now I am glad … but then I was still not in touch with or understanding the words of the Holy Spirit; banker?

Two Christian Girls

The doctors asked me why I jumped off the bridge. I told them, "I couldn't quit smoking cigarettes."

They didn't understand me, and at the time I didn't either. Ironically I found out months later that one of the girls who came to visit me the night before I dove off the bridge was having an affair with the minister. He was the one who told me he doubted if he could help me with my name on the blackboard as being unsaved. The church split up over the fiasco with the married minister's infidelity. Maybe life *is* like a box of chocolates.

I suffered at the hospital with my back now broken. Within a few days I was sent back to the mental hospital. They sent me to a lockup ward for punishment; I thought I had already punished myself.

The rooms were cold at night. I was rooming with criminals who committed various crimes, and I did not know what to do to get out of there. After about a week they let me out and I went back to the ward. Now I had to go and see another therapist! I told her about my youth with Jeff in bed, and she tried to sell me on the idea that I was a homosexual. Now my problems were really solved. She didn't take into account the fact that I liked sexual relations only with women. I was actually getting tired of discussing my past with therapists and doctors anyway.

After some time I quit going to see her. After going back to the open ward I made a commitment to God. In a group therapy session I promised that I would never try to kill myself again. I did not say that I could fix the rest of me but that I would not commit this sin. I have kept this oath to this day. I still continue to struggle trying to fix me, though. I starting going to the church at the hospital and even sang with my guitar at the services. I sang a lot of Simon and Garfunkel songs.

Look on my affliction and rescue me,
For I do not forget Your law.
Plead my cause and redeem me;
Revive me according to Your word.

Psalm 119:153–154

I did need reviving, in some manner or form …

Sharon and Elizabeth

Actually Sharon met me. I was lying on the couch at the hospital trying to find some peace within myself. She walked in and said she was my nurse. I told her that I had a relationship with my last nurse. She was amused. Willing to have another try at life, I started having conversations with her. You might say I was very codependent. I am starting to get humorous about my affliction now. My gift of perseverance also shows up here.

We developed a relationship, and I again left the hospital to visit her and again got in trouble. This time they were also on Sharon's back for having a relationship with a patient. Somehow all of this resolved itself in time. I also started working at the hospital, making seventy-five cents an hour washing dishes. I wanted to become a "banker."

I was then able to have my first experience with fatherhood. Sharon had a little three-year-old girl, Elizabeth, from her first marriage. She was very delicate. When I first saw her I was so proud of her, hoping and possibly wanting to become her father. Samantha had told me that she thought she was pregnant once. She said she was happy then. She told me this while we were in the divorce process. What a cruel thing to say at that time. Again words are like a sword to the heart with the power to kill.

I was discharged from the state mental hospital and went again back to my apartment in Milford. I then asked my parents if I could stay with them for a while. I had no money. I guess it would have made my life easier if I was a "banker." A repetitive prodigal son I was, with no keep or money.

My parents again agreed to allow me to stay with them. This time they slaughtered the cow and gave me my first birthday party at their house. I was twenty-nine years old, and I was overwhelmed. There were a lot of people there, even the old boyfriend of one of my sisters, whom she broke up with after high school. I felt so honored. When I listened to Bette Midler's song "Wind Beneath My Wings" I imagined this is how Jeff feels about me in heaven. I seriously believe that Jeff thinks I'm his hero.

He heals up the brokenhearted
And binds up their wounds.

P<small>SALM</small> **147:3**

Maybe just maybe I can put some closure to this!

Sharon's Family

I had begun a new life with a new nurse and her daughter and her family. Initially her family would not accept me because of my history with mental illness. I became low over this and had to make another stop at PSU to get on medicine again. They got me straightened out with Triliphon, and I was home in a record two weeks. I then went to work for a small oil company in Shelby, Ohio, to try to get back in the workforce. I filed and collected from Social Security disability again, which gave me some money to start on. In the coming years I went back to school part-time and even got promoted to full-time work. Things again were back on track and going well. I even applied for another job with another oil company. I was accepted at GNC Oilfield Company at Aurora, Ohio, and became their superintendent. I was somewhat happy again and seemed to have a future.

Chapter 6
1984–1991

*Train up a child in the way he should go,
Even when he is old he will not depart from it.*

PROVERBS 22:6

My Daughter Elise

I married Sharon and was blessed with a daughter, Elise, born on September 23, 1986. That same day I quit smoking cigarettes, the hardest addictive behavior I had ever conquered. I had crossed many bridges to get to this point.

I recall Sharon going into labor at about five thirty in the morning. I was very excited. I sped all the way to the hospital in Bradford, Ohio, about fifty miles away. Elise was born at around nine o'clock AM. She was beautiful. The only problem was that Sharon had trouble delivering the placenta. She was going into shock. I prayed on her head that she would be okay. The doctor finally delivered it and she recuperated. That evening the hospital gave us dinner together to celebrate Elise's birth. I was so proud of my second child.

Over the years I became very protective of Elise's well-being. I drove Sharon crazy with my demands. As she was growing up I took her for rides on my motorcycle. Actually this was a risk for me and her. She came to find peace on these rides even as she grew older. I had to give up riding with her, because of my age and arthritis in my later years.

*The fear of the Lord is the beginning of wisdom,
And the knowledge of the Holy One is understanding …*

                                                                                              PROVERBS 9:10

I came to fear God again and love Him as an understanding Father.

My Fourth Therapist

I worked at an oilfield company as a superintendent of 120 deep oil wells. I was happy being in charge of nine people. I was drilling wells and maintaining them. In 1989, through my father-in-law, I got an opportunity to work at Union Pacific. He became part owner of Union Pacific through his service years as a research and development leader and was now vice president in charge of sales. The transition from working with oil wells to molten metal was a large technical jump. I started out as a process control engineer and found the work rewarding but difficult. I met a good friend there who was a true metallurgist. I was able to advance at Union because of my problem-solving skills.

As time passed I started feeling low again and decided to search for another therapist. This time I searched for a Christian therapist in Avery, Ohio. I found a very sweet soul. I would tell her of my history and the way I felt. She would always take notes and reviewed my progress each session. It was a place I could freely talk about anything I wanted to. I always wanted to talk to my family about Jeff but couldn't. One time when I tried one of my twin sisters said, "You need to get by the past."

I was learning through therapy that you should deal with the past no matter how long ago it was. My sister was still covering up her feelings. My family then and now did not want to get together and talk about the accident and the events of that day. It's incredible!

I also was still on Triliphon from the PSU hospital and was still seeing the psychiatrist there too. After I talked of my issues with my Christian therapist we would pray together. I recall waking up one night at home to a voice up in the right corner of my bedroom that said, "*Aqui* gag," or was it, "A Key Greg"? I do not know. *Aqui* means "here" in Spanish. My therapist was initially unsure whether I was a Christian or not, but that changed in time, especially with the events after my father's death.

I had a very powerful dream one night. I was coming up out of the water that was inside a rock. I was crying heavily and said, "I am afraid to die." I looked up and saw a figure on a ledge that had steps behind it going up to a doorway in the rock in the upper-left corner. Light came from around the door. I approached the figure, who stood in a long white robe with long hair. I hugged him at the waist for he was on the ledge and I still was in shallow water. I awoke stunned.

CHAPTER 7
1991–1998

Death and life are in the power of the tongue,
And those who love it will eat its fruit.

PROVERBS 18:21

Again I believe words spoken to you can build you up or destroy you, especially when you are susceptible, as is a child growing up.

My Father's Death

My father started having heart problems in his early fifties. I remember lying on the couch watching him hold his chest as he rested in his recliner in my early years at home. In one instance after my dad had one of his heart attacks as I was driving home from the hospital, I looked to the right and back and told God I hated him. I did not like all the grief. I was tired of carrying it. I held this hatred toward God until after my father's death. I felt somewhat relieved saying I hated God at the time.

I later prayed that God would let me have Dad's illness to relieve him. He was soft-spoken in his later years and more at peace, but I believed that he feared death as I did. The night before he died Mother told me he was acting very strangely when he was driving her to town. I sat down with him on the porch and felt the heaviness of the situation. My awareness told me he was preparing to die. I told him not to take Mom with him. He knew what I meant about not driving. That night he did not sleep because of his heart. He had had many heart attacks since 1970. The doctors told him he would not make it through bypass surgery. The next morning he ate breakfast and at around 10:00 AM asked Eudora to take him to the hospital. My brother-in-law called me at the plant and said that dad had gone to the hospital. He died before I got there, and mother again was grieving in the ICU waiting room. I went back to see him;

he lay still on the bed. The veins of his lower jaw were blue from lack of oxygen. I lay next to him and cried and then looked up at the ceiling to the right and said, "I love you."

As he was traveling, it happened that he was approaching Damascus, and suddenly a light from heaven flashed around him.

Acts 9:3

I personally have experienced this road. The only difference was that the uttering of the Spirit in me opened my eyes and mind to Him. The experience did not blind my eyes as with Paul.

The Road to Sardis (Damascus)

The following morning I wanted to hide in bed. I struggled to face the day and determine what to do. I decided to go to my part-time consulting job in Sardis, Ohio, and check the oil wells. I first drove to the park along the river and sat in my truck crying and grieving heavily. After a while I started driving the fifteen-mile trip to the first well. I put in a Christian CD to listen to as I drove. About halfway there I was grieving and crying very heavily. Sobbing, I looked back to the right and up and said, "I love you."

At the time I'm not sure if I was talking to my father or to God or both. I quickly turned back to the road and drove on. As I was approaching Sardis I started to descend down a hill. There was a Baptist church on the left. My head then dropped and turned to the left and said something in an unknown language and then turned to the right and said, "Make me true in thought, word, and deed."

I speculate that the unknown language was Latin and the English portion was the interpretation. All this time I was observing myself do this from above my head. Was my soul splitting from my mind and body, or was my soul splitting from the Holy Spirit and body? I do not know. As this was settling down, I continued to drive to the wells. At that time the heavy grieving stopped and all my grief was gone.

We buried Dad the following day. Soon after this experience I wanted to tell someone of the experience on that road. While shopping one day I chose Sharon. Her comment was, "Do you think you're better than everyone else now?"

I immediately was brought low by her cruel words. Would a better comment have been that she was glad I had a godly experience? Did she really feel herself lowered by my experience? Wasn't I the one messed up? More cruel words …

Jesus said to them, 'A prophet is not without honor except in his hometown, and among his own relatives, and in his own household.'

MARK 6:4

'He who has believed and has been baptized shall be saved; but he who has disbelieved shall be condemned. These signs will accompany those who have believed: In My name they will cast out demons, they will speak with new tongues; they will pick up serpents, and if they drink any deadly poison, it will not hurt them; they will lay hands on the sick, and they will recover.'

MARK 16:16–18

Graduating from College

In the spring of 1992 I finally graduated from college. My niece, a generation behind me in age, graduated with me. My final GPA was 3.49. I had done well, but the road was long. A literature class kept me from graduating cum laude. I had taken the final that spring and had two questions out of five to write a theme on. With my newfound wisdom I incorporated two of the questions under one title. The instructor never caught it and gave me a 50 percent on the final. I went back to him and told him of his error. He said he had already submitted the grades and would not resubmit.

Upon graduation I had an offer from the oil company Unocal in Bakersfield, California. Sharon and I decided to fly out to check out the offer. I tried to negotiate with them to raise my salary offer but failed. Union had offered me more. I decided to remain with Union and stay in my hometown.

I continued to work at Union and became very successful with my process changes and inventions. I was promoted to product manager and then to plant manager. I enjoyed the job at Union, but it was very demanding and competitive and added to my stress level tremendously. I was somewhat overwhelmed.

In addition I took on the challenge of going to graduate school. I had been accepted in an EMBA program.

And the peace of God, which surpasses all comprehension, will guard your hearts and minds in Christ Jesus.

PHILIPPIANS 4:7

For me it took thirty-plus years …

Heart Surgery

During the spring of 1996 my sister Penny had heart surgery. She had a valve replaced and three bypasses. I remember praying with my brother-in-law for her recovery. Little did I know that she would survive and a little over a year later he would die of cancer of the stomach. My father-in-law also came down with Guillian-Barré syndrome, and Sharon quit work to take care of him.

At one point that same summer I overexerted myself physically one day and felt some burning in my upper chest. It lasted for several days. I finally went to Milford Hospital. They diagnosed me with acid reflux, but I was not satisfied with this. During the first part of the summer I had a stress test and physical at PSU. They said I was normal, but again I was not satisfied because of my father's experience with heart disease. I then got some of my older EKGs at Milford Hospital and sent them to a doctor at PSU to match with my most recent physical there. "Yes," a heart specialist said, "there is something happening within you." I was then scheduled for a heart catheterization. The heart catheterization showed major blockages everywhere, and they told me during the procedure that I would need surgery. They then scheduled me for surgery on my daughter Elise's birthday, September 23, 1996.

They told me I would have three bypasses, but while I was in surgery they decided to do four. They used all arteries on me and took one from my right arm. There were some complications after surgery with my chest x-rays while in post-op when they found what appeared to be a clot in my right lung. They thought that I would have to go back into surgery. There was a younger fellow on the other side of the room, and the nurse said he was dying. His family came to be with him, and I felt sorrow for him and his family and prayed for him. The doctor with me said he would take one more x-ray of my chest before they took me to surgery again. The clot had disappeared. I then got up and walked to a wheelchair with tubes hanging from me. Following surgery I went to a regular room. The doctors there wanted to get me home early but wanted to give me blood to do that. One doctor told me not to take it even if they insisted. I was forty-six years young and had not taken blood throughout the surgery. They actually kept me an extra day to get my blood count up.

I was discharged from the hospital and back home recuperating in six days. There I sensed a sun-like light in the upper corner of my bedroom while I was healing.

CHAPTER 8
1998–PRESENT

For a righteous man may fall seven times, and rises again …

PROVERBS 24:16

Here we go again and again and again …

My Second Divorce

In the late nineties after my heart surgery I decided to build Sharon and me our dream house in Milford, Ohio. After my heart surgery and newfound life I seemed to take on more risks. Sharon's parents gave us money to purchase the property to build a specially designed and made timber-frame home. It was very costly, though, and was stretching our budget, since I could not get my wife to go back to work consistently.

During the construction of the house she kept using the phrase "My father is an owner of Union." This made budgeting with contractors much worse. I finished the house way over budget, and we settled in. When Elizabeth decided to get married, we had the wedding at the house. Although it rained that day the wedding went very well and Elizabeth had a very good wedding with her new husband. I was able to find him a new place in my heart. His name was the same as my brother's. Both he and Elizabeth graduated from Milford Tech. They had degrees as a chef and an EMT. I was and am proud of both of them.

I tried to get Sharon to go back to work because of budget conditions. She did try a few jobs but ended up quitting them and took up a hobby talking to people on the Internet. This evolved into her sitting in front of the computer all day. Her dad got into arguments with the CEO of Union over a position change that I was forced into at work. I was very disappointed in my movement at work and needed to talk. I had asked her several times to talk with me, but she came down from the computer and said, "You got five minutes."

I became very upset over this and angry. One day I decided to cut the computer cord and did so. She found out about the cord obviously and threatened divorce.

I had to travel to Germany for Union and spent the next few months grieving over my second marriage. When I would call Sharon she would be very standoffish. I kept trying and trying to reason with her. I felt sorry for my daughter Elise, who was in grade school. How would this affect her? At one point she was at Elizabeth's apartment and was grieving over the situation of her mother and me breaking up. I felt so bad for her. She was in the eighth grade and so young to be hurt. After grieving myself over the situation and Sharon's hard stance about a divorce, I finally quit grieving over this. Two months was enough for feeling this low again. I decided to let her have the divorce and get it over with as quickly as possible. We met with an arbitrator and split up the assets. I got the house and no alimony. Elise stayed with her mother most of the time. I had to pay child support to my ex-wife now, though.

He who finds a wife finds a good thing
And obtains favor from the Lord.

Proverbs 18:22

I am not sure why I should not give up with women … I can't believe my own therapist thought I should be homosexual …

Reba

Upon giving up on Sharon, I went on the lookout for another companion. Since early childhood I always looked forward to having a wife. I needed someone to hold … like Jeff. I finally found Reba while I was in Germany, although she was from the states. I was like a teenager in love with her voice talking to her on the phone. I needed someone and I found her. I was most pleased with her being a Christian. I made arrangements to meet her in Morgantown, West Virginia. The first time I met her I grabbed her and kissed her. I gave her three roses, one red, one yellow, and one white, and some items from Germany. It was wonderful. We then drove to Charleston, West Virginia, and went to the mall.

Through the divorce with Sharon in the spring of 2001, I felt torn inside with my former family. I again felt low over the relationships now with my two daughters. Sharon won out with their relationship even though she instigated the divorce as a way to control me. I turned the other cheek and started over again with another person. I put my heart and soul into Reba.

Reba and I went away and got married a few years later. We have had a wonderful relationship even to this day. The Lord has blessed me with her and again through all my trials. We talk of the past and hold no issues when we discuss our feelings. We explore them and try and understand our ways. She is my lover and friend most of all. We do projects on her place and mine and plan for retirement with many things to do. My mother told me that if I was a girl when I was born she was going to name me Reba. One cannot find a better soul mate than this. Reba also has had issues with depression in her life. We relate to each other's needs and share experiences. I am greatly blessed with her presence in my life. She continues to live in Morgantown, West Virginia. I live in Milford, Ohio. We talk to each other daily and spend weekends together. I enjoy her immensely.

I will give You thanks with all my heart;
I will sing praises to You before the Gods.
I will bow down toward Your holy temple
And give thanks to Your name for Your loving kindness and
Your truth;
For You have magnified Your word according to all Your name.
On the day I called, You answered me;
You made me bold with strength in my soul.

Psalm 138:1–3

Reflections and Hope

After writing these chronicles I find myself looking at my past more objectively and with forgiveness. Jeff's death has left me with an anxiety to constantly rush to get tasks done, but now I recognize that and deal with it. I also seem to continually look for approval with my family. Even writing these chronicles I find myself wanting to distort the truth so as not to cause anxiety for my relatives. But I write my perspective on what I believe to be true, regardless of being offensive to some. In myself I find forgiveness for me and others, and this in no way cancels the love I feel for others.

I continue to suffer from anxiety and some melancholy, especially when I am alone. This mostly happens in the middle of the night when I am most weak in my rational thought. I still take medication for my mental condition, Lexapro and Zyprexa. When I am with Reba the symptoms are much less. I conclude that these scars will become less sensitive over time. I patiently await my eternal being and permanent healing covered by a white robe as the bride given to me by my groom Jesus Christ at the wedding supper of the lamb. I have not given up on Him, or, I believe, Him me.

My Christian life has not been ordinary. I have actually been mentally persecuted by some Christians and mentally hammered with law by the beliefs of others. My relationship with the Savior is personal, and that is all. I frown at the customs of most of the Christian organizations. I believe that they have driven a lot of people away from a personal relationship with their God. My own bond with Him has been tested in this atmosphere and still is. By writing of these events I have fulfilled my destiny relative to the events in my childhood. I have not waited for heaven to disclose what happened to me and will hold forgiveness as my trophy also. I also will continue to run the good race and await his arrival or my leaving this body permanently.

A Validation

All of my life the events I write of are documented in time and history reports. These reports include newspapers and hospital visits and treatments. I presently am seeing a psychiatrist in Milford, Ohio. He has all my medication records and history. What cannot be proven by documentation are the mystical experiences that I have had. My only witness to these is my Lord Jesus Christ, and with Him I leave this in "truth in thought, word, and deed."

'He who has found his life will lose it, and he who has lost his life for My sake will find it.'

MATTHEW 10:39

EPILOGUE
June 9, 2009

A few weeks ago I had an amazing dream. I was lying in a bed across from Jeff's and my old bedroom and telling one of my sisters about my dreams with people who had passed away in my family. My sister Penny was sitting on Jeff's and my old bed and was trying to get me to come out of bed. I eventually got up and was led downstairs by Eudora. The dream was very vivid and strong; almost a vision. As I went downstairs I passed a lot of my family and behold was staring at Jeff at an equal height. We hugged and then sat down in front of a Christmas tree in the kitchen. I was filled with joy and happiness, as was everyone else. My mother then handed me the old-style phone as if I was to answer it. I put it to my ear and said hello many times. No one answered. I then went outside to meet many people who were gathered. I did not see my first wife but was looking for her. I then found myself in a church that was hewn out of a rock. I understood that I was to give a speech and went up to the podium on the left side of the church. There were elder-type people coming to the front of the church and sitting down. I then got the impression that I was to read what was on a piece of paper handed to me by a person who came up to the front of the church. I could not read the writing but closed my eyes and said, "You must take Christ with you when you go into the world." This dream was so vivid that it took me several days to not feel the high that it gave me or the blessing that it gave me. I feel that part of me has resolved my anxieties over the accident.

November 2009

In early November I began a series of dreams in which I am talking to an older figure, like a grandfather or even maybe God. I recall expressing to Him many situations and being very honest with Him about my life. After awakening, I could recall only one detail that He said to me. He said, "Time is on your side."

ABOUT THE AUTHOR

The author of this true story has used a pen name to protect the privacy of his acquaintances and relatives and himself. The only true name in the story is that of his brother Jeff. The lives that have been affected by Shawn are many. To this day he holds down a demanding job and still uses the gift of problem solving in his work. He travels the world with his job, working with his gift. He resides in southeastern Ohio and enjoys fishing and hunting and his wife Reba. The scars of mental illness have become less sensitive with time but still remain scars.